# The Secret on the Mountain

Fairfield P.N.E.U. School
(Backwell) Ltd.,
Farleigh Road,
Backwell, Bristol.

© Copyright 1994 by Kevin Mayhew Ltd.

KEVIN MAYHEW LTD
Rattlesden  Bury St Edmunds
Suffolk  England
IP30 0SZ

OPENBOOK PUBLISHERS
205 Halifax Street
Adelaide
SA 5000
Australia

ISBN  0 86209 524 7
Catalogue No. 1108124

Printed in Great Britain

# The Secret on the Mountain

### Retold from Scripture by Susan Sayers
### and illustrated by Arthur Baker

Kevin Mayhew

If you had lived in Galilee about two thousand years ago, you would probably have met Jesus at work. He spent a lot of time making people better, talking with them and teaching them how to love one another.

Often, in the evening, or before the sun had got up, Jesus set off by himself into the mountains, to spend some time with God, his Father.

It was so peaceful here. The moon and the planets, and all the distant stars, are there because God has made them. And Jesus, standing on planet Earth, could share God's love which made it all.

(His love still keeps it going, even today!)

Sometimes Jesus would say a thank-you to his Father for the wonders of his world. Sometimes he talked to God about the people he loved and about their needs. And sometimes he just stood quietly, happy to be in God's company.

One day Jesus asked three of his friends to climb the mountain with him.

'But don't you need some time on your own, Jesus?' they asked. 'Not today,' Jesus said, 'I'd like you to come as well.'

James, John and Peter were very pleased to be asked. Together, they started to climb.

It was steep and rocky. Lizards blinked at them, and the dust felt gritty in their sandals. Peter was quite out of breath. 'Phew!' he gasped, mopping his head with his sleeve. 'Are we nearly at the top?'

'You can borrow my staff if you like,' said John, kindly. 'Think of the view we'll have at the top!' said James.

The view was fantastic. All the hills and valleys were stretched out far below, in the sunlight. There were tiny clusters of houses and trees. And the lake glinted, clear and blue, with dots of boats moving across it.

'Isn't God's world beautiful!' whispered James. Jesus smiled. 'It certainly is!' he agreed.

Then Jesus began to pray. He prayed with such love and such joy that his face was lit up and radiantly happy. Peter, James and John watched him in amazement – they had never seen anyone pray like this before. As they gazed at Jesus they saw God's light spread through his whole body. Everything about him shone.

Two men were standing with him now. They were Moses and Elijah (who had both been God's close friends during their lifetime).

Jesus was talking with them about how he would save the world by dying for it, before coming to life again for ever.

'We are being allowed to peep into heaven!' thought John. It made him feel very peaceful and very happy.

Peter wanted to hold on to this moment for ever. 'What a good thing we're here, Master,' he said, 'we could make three shelters – one for each of you!'

Just then, a bright cloud settled on the mountain. Out of the cloud came a voice, more powerful – and yet more gentle – than any voice they had ever heard.

Yes, it was the voice of God himself. 'This is my dear Son,' he said. 'I'm very pleased with him. Listen to what he tells you.'

John, Peter and James could hardly take in what was happening. The wonder of it all made them frightened. (After all, it's not every day you see the secrets of heaven!) They clung to each other, terrified.

Jesus walked over and put his arm round their shoulders. He looked his normal self now, and Moses and Elijah had gone. 'Don't be afraid,' said Jesus, softly.

The disciples were itching to tell everyone what they had seen. Jesus had other ideas.

As they scrambled down the steep mountain track he said to them, 'I don't want you to tell anyone this secret yet; wait until I have come back to life again. Then you can tell whoever you like.'

After seeing the light of heaven on the mountain, it was strange to see flustered crowds gathered in the valley. They all needed Jesus and felt lost without him.

'Please, Jesus, cure my daughter!'

'Jesus, my mother is ill – can you help?'

'Jesus, my son has fits, and your friends can't heal him. Will you make him better?'

Very soon, Jesus was back working among the people he loved. No wonder God had said he was pleased with his Son.

Peter, James and John never forgot the shining majesty of Jesus on that mountain. And they kept their promise: they didn't tell anyone the secret until after Jesus had come back to life. (And one day, at the end of time, we shall ALL see him in his shining glory!)

Note for parents:
This story can be found in
Matthew 17:1-8; Mark 9:2-9;
Luke 9:28-36; 2 Peter 1:16-18.